HOW TO TEACH
WORLD LITERATURE
STUDENT REVIEW
QUESTIONS AND TESTS

ELIZABETH MCCALLUM MARLOW

WESTBOW
PRESS®
A DIVISION OF THOMAS NELSON
& ZONDERVAN

WestBow Press books may be ordered through booksellers or by contacting:

WestBow Press
A Division of Thomas Nelson & Zondervan
1663 Liberty Drive
Bloomington, IN 47403
www.westbowpress.com
1 (866) 928-1240

ISBN: 978-1-9736-3151-4 (sc)
ISBN: 978-1-9736-3152-1 (e)

Print information available on the last page.

WestBow Press rev. date: 06/23/2018

To the Teacher

The following review questions and tests are designed to be used in conjunction with *How to Teach World Literature: A Practical Teaching Guide*. All review questions and tests are included in the teaching guide and reproduced in this booklet with answers omitted.

Review questions

Copy and distribute a set of review questions to your class. Students break into small groups and refer to their literature books and notes as each group answers the questions. Every student answers the questions in his or her notebook. On an assigned day, students hand in their notebooks with the completed questions for grading. At a later date, the teacher should review with the class appropriate answers to each set of review questions. The teacher may choose to use some of the questions on tests and semester exams.

Tests

Test procedure[1]

    A. Taking tests[2]

Have students clear their desks and take out a pen. Distribute tests. Require students to place a cover sheet on top of their tests and move it down to cover answers as they take the test. The teacher may also wish to arrange students' desks at some distance apart. Instruct students to use the back of the test if they require more space for their responses. As students finish a test, they should place it face down on their desks and work on other assignments until everyone has completed the test. Collect the tests.

    B. Reviewing tests

Distribute graded tests and review answers. While grading the tests, the teacher may opt to note down excellent responses and ask individual students to read those responses to the class. Take time to answer students' questions about both questions and responses.

---

[1] I have found the following procedures to be effective. Other teachers may prefer to adopt methods that are more suited to the needs of a particular class.

[2] Some tests require the teacher to copy certain excerpts or poems and attach them to the back of the test.

Literature holds up a mirror to life

and in so doing allows us to better

understand ourselves and others.

Contents

Review questions on the *Iliad*

Name _____

1. Summarize the event that caused the Trojan War.

2. Define Hector's main conflict as he says goodbye to his wife. Be sure to include both sides of his dilemma.

3. Explain the symbolism of Hector's removing his helmet in the scene with his wife and son. Mention the names of his wife and son.

4. Greek boys read the *Iliad* in order to learn about their culture's values. What values do you think the two excerpts we read would have taught them?

5. Briefly mention two or three instances of divine intervention.

6. What part does Deiphobus play in the excerpts you read?

7. Who of the gods is Hector's champion and who is Achilles's champion?

8. What pleas does Hector's father make to motivate his son to return within the walls of Troy? Mention his name.

9. Why does Achilles refuse to fight in the Trojan War for a long period of time?

10. Why does Achilles finally decide to return to the battle?

11. Summarize Achilles's actions as he kills Hector.

12. Explain why Hector is a much more sympathetic character than Achilles. Do not supply information provided in previous answers.

13. What did the ancient Greeks think about Fate?

14. What did they believe about life after death?

15. What was the role of women in ancient Greece?

16 – 20: Name the people or gods described here:

_____ "the dread goddess"

"_____ of the strong ash spear."

"_____ of the white arms"

"swift-footed brilliant _____."

"tall _____ of the shining helm."

Review questions on *Antigone*

Name _____

1. What is the function of the chorus?

2. Explain how the play explores the conflict between political expedience and religious conviction.

3. What is Sophocles's position on the issue?

4. Briefly describe the differences in Antigone and Ismene's personalities.

5. What is Creon's tragic flaw?

6. How is Creon's flaw manifested throughout events of the play?

7. What advice does Haimon attempt to give his father?

8. Does this play adhere to the principle of decorum? Why or why not?

9. How does Creon attempt to absolve himself of responsibility for Antigone's death?

10. What is Teiresias's function in this play?

11. What prophecy does Teiresias make before he leaves Creon?

12. Is Antigone a static or dynamic character? Explain.

13. Does Creon experience anagnorisis or not? Explain.

14. Does the plot fulfill Aristotle's criteria for tragic drama? Explain.

15. Do you feel a certain amount of pity and fear for Antigone? for Creon?

16. Does either Antigone or Creon experience peripeteia or a reversal of fortune?

17. Do both main characters meet Aristotle's criteria for the tragic hero? Explain.

Review questions on the *Aeneid*

Name _____

1. Mention some major facts you have learned about Virgil and his epic.

2. Virgil begins his epic _____. (fill in the blank)

3. Where does Aeneas begin and end his journey?

4. Name the children of Priam and Hecuba.

5. At the beginning of Book 2, the Greek army divides into two groups. Where are both groups of soldiers?

6. What is Sinon's explanation for running away from the Greeks?

7. How does Sinon account for the presence of the wooden horse outside the walls of Troy?

8. What makes Sinon's account so convincing?

9. Who warns the Trojans about the wooden horse?

10. Who strikes the wooden horse and why does he/she take this action?

11. Summarize the horrific incident involving Laocoön.

12. What is the Trojans' reaction to this incident?

13. Why is Laocoön's fate ironic?

14. Name one or two famous warriors who hide inside the horse.

15. Whom does Aeneas see in a dream?

16. What instructions does that person give Aeneas?

17. Who escapes from Troy with Aeneas?

Review questions on *The Metamorphoses*

Name _____

1. Explain how Ovid's title, *The Metamorphoses*, applies to two people in the myths we read.

2. Name several themes explored in the myth of "Daedalus and Icarus."

3. Refer to Auden's poem entitled "The Shield of Achilles." What type of artwork does Thetis expect to see depicted on her son's shield? What pictures does Hephaestus, in fact, carve on the shield?

4. Look at the second stanza of Auden's poem. Comment on the poet's references to the prisoners.

5. Why would the ragged urchin be indifferent to violent acts?

6. Refer to the myth of "Orpheus and Eurydice." Who is Orpheus?

7. Why is Orpheus able to persuade the king and queen of Hades to allow his wife to return to earth?

8. Explain the tragic ending of the "Orpheus and Eurydice" myth.

9. Shakespeare used one of Ovid's myths for the plot of an entire play. Name the play.

10. Explain how Shakespeare makes comic use of the same Ovid myth in another play. Which version of that myth did you prefer—Ovid's or Shakespeare's? Explain your preference.

11. Explain the irony involved in the deaths of Pyramus and Thisbe.

12. Refer to the myth "Echo and Narcissus." Who is Nemesis and how do we use that word today?

13. Explain what is meant when someone is described as being narcissistic.

14. How does Echo anger the gods? What is her punishment?

15. Summarize the stories of Arachne and Midas. In terms of the myth, does Arachne deserve her fate? Does Midas? Why or why not?

16. Supply and define two well-known words that derive from the myths of Arachne and Midas.

Review questions on the *Inferno, The Decameron*, and *The Acts of King Arthur and His Noble Knights*

Name _____

the *Inferno*.

  1. What does Dante's Wood of Error symbolize?

  2. Why is the *Inferno* classified as a comedy?

  3. Briefly describe the two people who guide Dante through the three locations of the *Divine Comedy*.

  4. Define syncretism and explain why it is a false belief.

  5. How does Dante combine classical mythology with the Bible?

The Decameron

  6. Name two writers who were influenced by Boccaccio's tales.

  7. Give several valid reasons for the enduring popularity of "Patient Griselda"?

  8. List the three tests to which Gualtieri subjects Griselda.

9. How can one refute each reason for the tests to which Gualtieri subjected Griselda?

10. What is magnanimous about Monna's behavior in "Federigo's Falcon"?

11. What is one of Federigo's faults? and Monna's?

The Acts of King Arthur and His Noble Knights

12. Define the romance as a literary genre.

13. What was feudalism?

14. Name three characteristics of a chivalrous knight.

15. In romances, the hero often had a mysterious origin. Apply this trait to Steinbeck's retelling of Arthurian legends.

16. Who was Sir Kay?

17. List ways in which Steinbeck depicts Arthur as a chivalric knight even at the tender age of fifteen.

Review questions on *The Prince* and *The Adventures of Don Quixote*

Name _____

The Prince

1. What appears to have been Machiavelli's opinion of human nature?

2. What was Machiavelli's purpose for writing his treatise on statesmanship? Why was such a treatise necessary?

3. What was Machiavelli's main concept? Apply that concept to a ruler.

4. Name two or three examples Machiavelli provides of men who made good use of opportunities that came their way.

5. What was his caveat for new rulers?

6. In what ways does Machiavelli suggest that a ruler should disregard Christian principles?

The Adventures of Don Quixote

7. Define satire.

8. Give several examples of the way Cervantes satirizes romance as a literary genre.

9. Sancho Panza is a perfect foil for the Don. Name several differences in the characters of Don Quixote and his squire.

10. Summarize the famous windmill episode.

Review questions on *Julius Caesar*

Name _____

Act I

1. Differentiate between the two main conspirators' motivations for killing Caesar.

2. Provide one or two adjectives that summarize Cassius's personality.

3. Name two or three of Caesar's character flaws.

4. What stratagem does Cassius use to persuade Brutus to join the conspiracy?

Act II

5. Why are soliloquies important?

6. List Brutus's errors in the play so far.

7. Give one reason for Shakespeare's including the scene between Brutus and Portia.

8. How does Decius persuade Caesar to come to the Capitol?

Act III

9. What pretext do the conspirators use to gather closely around Caesar in order to assassinate him?

10. Why does Brutus command the conspirators to walk around with Caesar's blood smeared on their hands?

11. Name three of Antony's rhetorical tricks during his speech at Caesar's funeral.

12. Why does Shakespeare include the scene depicting the murder of Cinna the poet?

Act IV

13. Name two reasons why Caesar remains a vital presence in the play after his assassination.

14. What is one function of the quarrel scene between Brutus and Cassius?

15. How does Portia die and what is Brutus's reaction to her death?

16. What does Caesar's ghost prophesy?

Act V

17. Explain the symbolism of the eagles and scavenger birds that Cassius sees at Philippi.

18. Explain what Titinius means when he says of Cassius, "Alas, thou hast misconstrued everything!"

19. How do we know that Brutus inspires great loyalty?

20. Mention some facts that are different about the deaths of Cassius and Brutus.

21. Why does Shakespeare give Octavius the closing lines of the play?

Review questions on Jean de La Fontaine's *Fables* and Molière's *Tartuffe*

Name _____

the *Fables*

1. Write out the moral of "The Council Held by the Rats."

2. What clever additional detail does La Fontaine add to the ending of the well-known fable "The Hare and the Tortoise"?

3. Think about "The Fox and the Grapes." How do Aesop's and La Fontaine's morals differ?

4. In the fable that features a cicada and an ant, why is the ant unsympathetic to the cicada's need for help? With whom do you sympathize? Explain.

5. What is satiric about the moral of "The Crow and the Fox"?

6. The fable of the wolf and the lamb declares that might is right, but it illustrates the opposing position. Explain.

7. Explain the moral in the fable of "The Fox and the Stork."

Tartuffe

8. Explain how one character in this play embodies the traits of the Enlightenment period.

9. What is Madame Pernelle's function in this play?

10. Why is Damis concerned about his sister's marrying Tartuffe?

11. Explain how a maid such as Dorine is able to be involved in the family's concerns.

12. What is the basis of the absurd quarreling between Marianne and Valère in Act II scene iv?

13. Before we meet Tartuffe, we strongly suspect that he is a hypocrite. Why do we suspect this?

14. When we first meet Tartuffe, why are we certain that he is a religious hypocrite?

15. How does Molière convey Orgon's irrational character?

16. How does Tartuffe react to being told that he rather than Damis is Orgon's heir?

17. Explain how Madame Pernelle's continued admiration of Tartuffe is poetic justice for Orgon.

18. Did you enjoy this play? Explain your reaction.

Review questions on *Silas Marner*

Name _____

1. To what extent is this novel like a fairy tale?

2. Explain how Marner suffers prior to his coming to Raveloe.

3. Why are the inhabitants of Raveloe suspicious of Marner when he first arrives in their village?

4. Why does the loss of Marner's gold initiate contact between him and his neighbors?

5. Why is Dunstan a despicable person?

6. Why is Nancy Lammeter an exemplary person?

7. Briefly explain your opinion of Squire Cass.

8. Explain your opinion of Godfrey Cass.

9. List several of the novel's coincidences. Did they lessen your enjoyment of the book?

10. List several parallels between the two plots.

Review questions on 19th century and 20th century short fiction units

Name _____

"The Tell-Tale Heart," Edgar Allan Poe

1. Think about Poe's horror story. What issue does the first-person perspective raise? Explain your response.

2. How does Poe make it clear that the narrator is indeed insane?

3. Why did the murderer confess his crime?

4. Do you think the police suspect that a crime has been committed? Explain.

"The Bet," Anton Chekhov

5. Why does the lawyer in Chekhov's story read so indiscriminately during his last two years in prison?

6. Explain the differences in the characters of the banker and the lawyer in Chekhov's story.

7. List the various conflicts in this story.

"How Much Land Does a Man Need?" Leo Tolstoy

8. In one sentence, state Tolstoy's theme that the story illustrates.

9. Explain how this theme is developed via the protagonist's character.

10. Summarize Pahom's dream in Part 7 and explain its function.

"The Piece of String," Guy de Maupassant

11. Summarize the main character traits of the Norman peasants who live in Goderville.

12. What is your opinion of these peasants?

13. Identify the conflicts in this story. Are they external or internal conflicts?

"With All Flags Flying," Anne Tyler

14. What is the function of the following minor characters: Francie, Lollie Simpson, Mr. Pond?

15. Why is Tyler's title an appropriate choice for this story?

16. Why does Tyler describe Mr. Carpenter's traveling to his daughter's home on a motorbike?

"The Silver Mine," Selma Lagerlöf

17. Explain why this story is a frame narrative.

18. What is your opinion of the parson? Explain how he resolves the situation that arises after finding the silver mine.

19. Identify the dramatic irony in this story.

20. Is the king a static or dynamic character? Explain.

"The House on Mango Street," Sandra Cisneros

21. What is the meaning of the great-grandmother's looking out of the window for the rest of her life?

22. What universal truths does Cisneros convey with her sketches entitled "A Rice Sandwich" and "Chanclas"?

23. What central idea does Cisneros convey in "Mango Says Goodbye Sometimes"?

"Where have you gone, Charming Billy?" Tim O'Brien

24. Briefly explain the significance of the title.

25. This story describes a specific situation, a new recruit's initiation into war, but what universal experience does the story convey?

26. Why is the soldier's giggling realistic?

27. What is ironic about O'Brien's use of the well-known song in a story about war?

"The Pit and the Pendulum," Edgar Allan Poe

28. Summarize the facts you have learned about this story's setting.

29. Explain how this story can be read symbolically.

30. Why is it appropriate to label the close of this story a *deus ex machina* ending?

"Elias," Leo Tolstoy

31. What is the paradox illustrated in Tolstoy's story "Elias"?

"The Verger," W. Somerset Maugham

    32. Why was Albert Foreman's illiteracy a problem for the new vicar and the wardens of the church?

    33. What is your opinion of Albert Foreman? of the new vicar and church wardens?

Review questions on *A Separate Peace*

Name _____

1. Identify the novel's setting, both time and place.

2. What major literary device does Knowles adopt to tell this story?

3. Is Gene a reliable narrator? Why or why not?

4. List three opposing traits in Gene and Finny's personalities.

5. Name several major symbols in this novel and explain their symbolic function.

6. Why is it significant that Finny opens the winter carnival by burning a copy of the *Iliad*?

7. What false assumption does Gene make about Finny?

8. Why is it accurate to say that, to some extent, Leper is Finny's foil?

9. Why does Gene refuse to listen to details of Leper's disgrace?

10. What is Brinker's function?

11. What is Mr. Hadley's function?

12. Why does Finny believe in his friend and forgive Gene so readily for the suffering Gene has caused him?

13. Is Finny's second fall an accident? Why or why not?

14. Explain why Gene is the protagonist of this novel.

Review questions on *To Kill a Mockingbird*

Name _____

1. Briefly identify the following:

   a. Miss Stephanie Crawford

   b. Link Deas

   c. Mr. Gilmer

   d. Mr. Underwood

   e. Tim Johnson

   f. Charles Baker Harris

   g. Mrs. Grace Merriweather

   h. Dolphus Raymond

   i. Walter Cunningham

2. This novel is a *bildungsroman* or a novel about growing up. Mention three things Scout and Jem learn that teach them valuable lessons about courage.

3. Identify the structural device that unifies the book.

4. What does Atticus mean when he tells his children not to kill mockingbirds?

5. The novel consists of two parts that focus on people both black and white who are mockingbirds. Explain why these people can be called mockingbirds.

6. What one event brings the two parts together?

7. Explain how Harper Lee implicitly criticizes America's educational methods in the early twentieth century.

8. Why is Aunt Alexandra's tea party a sustained piece of irony?

9. List some times when Scout and Jem step into other people's skin in order to understand them.

10. What events cause Jem to finally understand why Arthur Radley does not care to socialize with his neighbors?

11. Where and when does Scout meet Arthur?

12. Why does Lee switch the perspective at the end of the novel?

13. Supply some reasons why every generation of young people should read *To Kill a Mockingbird*.

Review questions on the poetry unit

Name _____

Some questions are based on poetry you have not already read.

1 – 5: Read the following five passages and label the imagery in each one:

1. You spotted snakes with double tongue,
    Thorny hedgehogs, be not seen;
    Newts and blind-worms, do no wrong,
    Come not near our fairy queen…. (*A Midsummer Night's Dream,* Shakespeare)

2. I heard a Fly buzz—when I died….
    And then it was
    There interposed a Fly—
    With blue—uncertain stumbling Buzz…. ("I heard a Fly buzz," Emily Dickinson)

3. I came into the kitchen and bit into a slice of mom's savory apple pie, plump with juicy, sugary fruit.

4. Sometimes whoever seeks abroad may find
    Thee [autumn]…
    Drowsed with the fume of poppies….
    Or by a cidar-press, with patient look,
    Thou watchest the last oozings, hours by hours…. ("To Autumn," John Keats)

5. We tucked the baby into his warm blanket with his soft teddy bear.

6. Think about George Herbert's poem "Redemption." What do these people symbolize: the landlord; his tenant?

7. List the various meanings of the word "shadow" in "Eldorado" by Edgar Allan Poe.

8. Refer to "There is no frigate like a book" and list words Dickinson uses that connotatively convey the thrill of reading.

9. Refer to Jacques's speech in *As You Like It* that begins with this line: "All the world's a stage." What type of figurative language does Shakespeare employ throughout this speech?

10. Comment on the life lesson one learns by reading William Blake's poem entitled "The Poison Tree."

11 – 13: Identify the poetic devices in these lines:

11. "fluttering and dancing in the breeze…tossing their heads in sprightly dance."

12. "ten thousand saw I at a glance…"

13. "Beat! beat! drums! —blow! bugles! blow!
Through the windows—through doors—burst like a ruthless force…
So fierce you whirr and pound, you drums—so shrill you bugles blow.…"

14. Briefly describe how Lucille Clifton's "Miss Rosie" and Edna St. Vincent Millay's mother described in "The courage that my mother had" exhibit similar personalities.

15. What is the main regret of Edgar Lee Masters's speaker in the poem "George Gray"?

16. Identify the extended metaphor in Dickinson's poem that begins, "'Hope' is the thing with feathers."

17. What is the main poetic device in these lines by Walter de la Mare:
    Slowly, silently now the moon
    Walks the night in her silver shoon;
    This way, and that, she peers, and sees
    Silver fruit upon silver trees.

18. What poetic device does the poet use in this line: "Milton! Thou shouldst be living at this hour"?

19. What type of imagery is contained in these lines:
    And there lay the steed with his nostril all wide,
    But through it there rolled not the breath of his pride;
    And the foam of his gasping lay white on the turf,
    And cold as the spray of the rock-beating surf.

    And there lay the rider distorted and pale,
    With the dew on his brow, and the rust on his mail [armor]. . ..

20. What sound devices are used in these lines:
    The splendor falls on castle walls
    And snowy summits old in story;
    The long light shakes across the lakes. . ..

21. Explain why John Masefield's particular choice of meter enhances the meaning of his poem entitled "Sea Fever."

22. A poem by Lawrence Ferlinghetti begins thus: "Constantly risking absurdity." What main idea is explored in this poem?

23. We read a brief poem by Edna St. Vincent Millay that begins, "My candle burns at both ends." What is its tone?

24. What is the tone of "Theme for English B"?

25. What is the theme of Thomas Hardy's poem entitled "The Children and Sir Nameless"?

26. Explain how another poet explores the same theme.

Greek Literature Test

Name _____

the *Iliad*, Homer

1. Summarize the cause of the Trojan war.

2. Name the god who is Hector's champion and the god who is Achilles's champion.

3. List several reasons Hector's wife gives her husband for staying within the walls of Troy rather than returning to the battlefield.

4. What is Hector's principal motivation for returning to the battle in order to fight the Greeks?

5. What were the ancient Greeks' ideas about the following: Fate, the afterlife, the role of women?

6. How is it decided that Achilles will defeat Hector?

7. Why is Hector's death inevitable?

8. As he dies, what last request does Hector ask of Achilles? Does Achilles honor the request? Explain.

9. What advantages did Greek boys gain from reading Homer's epics?

10. Based on the excerpts you read, what is your opinion of Hector? of Achilles?

Fables, Aesop

11. Summarize what you know about Aesop and his *Fables.*

12. List some everyday expressions that are derived from Aesop's *Fables.*

Antigone, Sophocles

13. Name the main conflict that the play explores. What is the playwright's position on the issue?

14. Explain why Ismene is a foil character.

15. How does Sophocles's play demonstrate the far-reaching effects of Oedipus's sins?

16. Who is Teiresias and what is his function in this play?

17. Do you sympathize with Antigone? with Creon? Explain your opinions.

18. In your opinion, who is the play's protagonist? Defend your choice.

19. What is your opinion about the function of the chorus?

"Death of Socrates," from the *Phaedo,* Plato

20 – 22: Define these three terms:

  20. Socratic method

  21. sophistry

  22. dialogue

23. Based on Plato's dialogue describing Socrates's death, mention several reasons why it is accurate to call Socrates a virtuous pagan.

"Allegory of the Cave," from the *Republic*

24. In a sentence or two, explain Plato's belief about reality. Briefly explain how the poster assignment helped you to understand Plato's theory.

the *Poetics*, Aristotle

25 – 27: Define these principles from Aristotle's *Poetics:*

    25. catharsis

    26. tragic hero

    27. anagnorisis

28. In your opinion, should tragic dramatists follow Aristotle's principle of decorum? Why or why not?

Roman Literature Test

Name _____

Aeneid, **Virgil**

1. What is Aeneas's main character trait? What is his mission?

2. Identify these characters: Capys, Dido, Sinon, Cassandra, Laocoön.

3. What pretext do the Greeks give the Trojans for the presence of the wooden horse outside Troy?

4. How do the Greeks persuade the Trojans to drag the horse into the city of Troy?

5. What is Laocoön's reaction to the Greeks' explanation about the horse?

6. What happens to Laocoön?

7. In the excerpt we read, whom does Aeneas see in a dream, and what instructions is he given? Does Aeneas obey these instructions?

The Metamorphoses, **Ovid**

8 – 11: Name the metamorphosis in each of these myths:

    8. "Daedalus and Icarus"

9. "Echo and Narcissus"

10. "Arachne"

11. "Pyramus and Thisbe"

"Daedalus and Icarus"

12. What details in Brueghel's painting *Landscape with the Fall of Icarus* convey mankind's indifference to people's suffering?

13. Poets have often explored this theme of indifference to suffering. Provide the title and author of one or two poems that deal with the theme.

"Echo and Narcissus"

14. Why is Narcissus cursed and what is the result of the curse?

"Orpheus and Eurydice"

15. Name some examples of residents in Hades who are lured by Orpheus's irresistible music. What is each person's fate in Hades?

"Arachne"

16. Why is Arachne punished so severely?

"Pyramus and Thisbe"

17. Why are the lovers' deaths ironic?

18. Briefly explain how Shakespeare transforms Ovid's serious love story into comedy during the final scene of *A Midsummer Night's Dream*.

Medieval Literature Test

Name _____

The Decameron, Boccaccio

1. Identify the story-telling device Boccaccio uses for his collection of short stories and explain why it is a useful device for a short story writer. Mention another writer who has used the device.

2. Explain how Boccaccio uses the story-telling device.

"Patient Griselda"

3. List the various tests to which the Marquis subjects Griselda.

4. List two of the Marquis's reasons for the tests.

5. Explain why the Marquis's tests are unnecessary.

"Federigo's Falcon"

6. What character trait does this story illustrate? Explain how Boccaccio uses the falcon to symbolize the virtue the story illustrates.

7. Write out one <u>social</u> and one <u>moral</u> problem that Monna Giovanna faces when her son asks her to obtain the falcon.

8. Are the characters of either Federigo or Monna without fault?

Inferno, Dante

9. One of Dante's guides during two books of the *Divine Comedy* is the Roman poet Virgil. What does Dante intend Virgil to symbolize? Who is Dante's guide in the third book? What does he or she symbolize?

10. Summarize the facts you know about Dante's version of hell. What spiritual truth is conveyed by the poet's description of hell?

11. Explain why the *Divine Comedy* is a comedy.

12. Why is it also an allegory?

13. At the beginning of the epic, Dante is lost in a wood. What does this circumstance symbolize?

The Acts of King Arthur and His Noble Knights, Steinbeck

14. How does Steinbeck remain faithful to the idea that a romantic hero has a mysterious origin?

15. Give several reasons why it is accurate to state that Arthur is the quintessential knight.

16. What is Sir Kay's relationship to Arthur? Explain how Sir Kay is a foil character.

17. What was Steinbeck's purpose in writing his version of the Arthurian legends?

Renaissance Literature Test (excluding *Julius Caesar*)

Name _____

The Prince, Machiavelli

1. What was Machiavelli's purpose in writing *The Prince*?

2. What is the point of Machiavelli's analogy concerning archers?

3. Summarize what Machiavelli has to say about the importance of opportunity. Machiavelli cites several men in order to lend weight to his contention. List several of these men.

4. What does Machiavelli have to say about the use of force?

5. Write out Machiavelli's main idea. Explain what is meant by the term "Machiavellian."

The Adventures of Don Quixote, Cervantes

6. Having read many books of chivalrous romance, what decision does the Don reach?

7. List the preparations the Don makes before carrying out that decision.

8. Summarize the famous windmills episode.

9. How does the Don explain his defeat in this episode?

10. What is amusing about the Don's insistence that Sancho may not defend him unless he is attacked by common people?

11. How is Sancho a foil for the Don?

12. What are the meanings of these expressions: "quixotic"; "tilting at windmills"?

13. Is there anything you found to admire about Don Quixote? Explain your opinion.

Julius Caesar Acts I–III Test

Name _____

1. Provide a detailed summary of the play's historical background. What was Shakespeare's source for this play?

2. Write notes on the important information Shakespeare provides in the opening scene.

3 – 12: State the <u>speaker</u> and <u>something significant</u> about the following passages:

3. Why, man, he doth bestride the narrow world
    Like a Colossus, and we petty men
    Walk under his huge legs and peep about
    To find ourselves dishonorable graves.

Speaker:

Significance:

4. Well, —— thou are noble; yet I see
    Thy honorable mettle may be wrought
    From that it is disposed. . ..

Speaker:

Significance:

5. . . . 'tis common proof
    That lowliness [humility] is young ambition's ladder,
    Whereto the climber upward turns his face;
    But when he once attains the upmost round,
    He then unto the ladder turns his back,
    Looks in the clouds, scorning the base degrees [low rungs of the ladder]

By which he did ascend.

Speaker:

Significance:

6. . . . . upon my knees
    I charm [beg] you, by my once commended beauty,
    By all your vows of love, and that great vow
    Which did incorporate and make us one,
    That you unfold to me, your self, your half,
    Why you are heavy, and what men tonight
    Have had resort to you.

Speaker:

Significance:

7. Your statue spouting blood in many pipes,
    In which so many smiling Romans bathed. . .
    Signifies that. . . great men shall press
    For tinctures, stains, relics and cognizance [acknowledgment].

Speaker:

Significance:

8. . . . I am as constant as the Northern Star,
    Of whose true-fixed and resting [changeless] quality
    There is no fellow [equal] in the firmament.

Speaker:

Significance:

9. Stoop, Romans, stoop,
   And let us bathe our hands in —— 's blood
   Up to the elbows, and besmear our swords.

Speaker:

Significance:

10. O pardon me, thou bleeding piece of earth,
    That I am meek and gentle with these butchers!

Speaker:

Significance:

11. Romans, countrymen, and lovers, hear me for my cause, and be silent, that you may hear.

Speaker:

Significance:

12. If you have tears, prepare to shed them now.

Speaker:

Significance:

13. In his plays, Shakespeare emphasizes the importance of order throughout the land. How does Shakespeare convey the breakdown in order in this play?

14. Mention several rhetorical devices that Mark Antony uses during his funeral oration honoring Caesar that he delivers before the plebeians.

15. Why does Shakespeare include the scene depicting Cinna's murder?

Julius Caesar Acts IV–V Test

Name _____

1. When Brutus and Cassius quarrel, what accusations does Brutus level at his friend?

2. What does Cassius say about Brutus's military ability?

3. Brutus and Cassius argue over military strategy. What reasons does Cassius give for remaining at Sardis rather than moving on to Philippi? Does Cassius's opinion prevail? Why or why not?

4. List some of the ways in which Caesar remains a presence in the play after his assassination.

5. What does Shakespeare imply when he has Lucilius impersonate Brutus during the battle scenes?

6. Summarize the differences in the characters of Brutus and Cassius and their differing motives for killing Caesar.

7. Does Brutus regret joining the conspiracy and killing Caesar? Explain.

8 – 11: State the <u>speaker</u> and <u>something significant</u> about the following passages:

8. This is a slight unmeritable man
   Meet to be sent on errands.

Speaker:

Significance:

9.   . . . thou shalt see me at Philippi.

Speaker:

Significance:

10. . . . this same day
    Must end that work the ides of March begun;
    And whether we shall meet again I know not.
    Therefore our everlasting farewell take
    Forever, and forever, farewell. . ..

Speaker:

Significance:

11. This was the noblest Roman of them all. . ..
    His life was gentle, and the elements
    So mixed in him that Nature might stand up
    And say to all the world, "This was a man!"

Speaker:

Significance:

12. How and why does Portia die? How does Brutus react to the news of her death?

13. Give some valid reasons for the quarrel scene.

14. Having read the play, what is your personal opinion of Brutus?

15. Who gives a eulogy for Brutus at the end of the play?

16. Who speaks the closing lines, and why is this character the most appropriate person to close the play?

17. In as much detail as possible, summarize your opinion of Shakespeare's Caesar.

19th Century and Modern Short Fiction Test

Name_____

"The Bet," Anton Chekhov

1. What are the stipulations of the bet?

2. Why does the lawyer agree to it?

3. After his long, involuntary imprisonment, what does the lawyer conclude about life?

4. What is your opinion about the issue of capital punishment versus life imprisonment?

5. In one sentence, suggest a possible theme for this story.

"The Tell-Tale Heart," Edgar Allan Poe

6. In your opinion, why has this gruesome tale remained so popular among readers of horror fiction?

7. List some ways in which Poe creates suspense. Do not repeat information you may have provided in the previous question.

8. To what extent does guilt play a part in this story?

"How Much Land Does a Man Need?" Leo Tolstoy

9. Think about the Faust myth in which the devil lures a man into selling his soul for some sort of gain. Explain how Tolstoy's story is another version of the Faust myth.

10. How does Pahom's attitude to land differ from that of the Bashkir chief?

11. How does this story reflect Tolstoy's beliefs about private ownership of property?

12. Write out a one-sentence theme for this story. Briefly explain how Tolstoy develops this central idea.

"The Piece of String," Guy de Maupassant

13. List some character traits that define the French peasants.

14. When Hauchecorne continues to protest his innocence, his protestations have the opposite effect. Explain.

15. State the story's external and internal conflicts.

"The Verger," W. Somerset Maugham

16. What is the central irony of this story?

17. Is the irony in Maugham's story verbal, dramatic, or situational?

18. Provide a few of the verger's main personality traits. Give his full name.

"The Silver Mine," Selma Lagerlöf

19. Provide two adjectives that define the personality of the king.

20. Why does the king's attitude change at the end of the story?

21. What effect does the silver mine's discovery have on the four hunters who, along with the parson, discover the silver mine?

22. Explain why the parson is a wise man.

23. Define the contrast the author makes between the two main characters in this story. Explain whether the king is a dynamic or a static character.

"With All Flags Flying," Anne Tyler

24. How does Lollie Simpson relate to the title of this story?

25. Why did the writer include Mr. Pond in the story?

26. How does Francie's character help us understand her grandfather's dilemma?

27. What is this story's theme?

"The Pit and the Pendulum," Edgar Allan Poe

28. Provide a detailed description of the various horrors the prisoner encounters in this tale.

29. How does the prisoner escape the menace of the rats?

30. What is your reaction to the ending?

31. Define the story's symbolic meaning. What details support this reading?

"Where Have You Gone, Charming Billy?" Tim O'Brien

32. Briefly provide some historical background for this story. From what perspective is the story written?

33. Comment on the ironic title.

"The House on Mango Street," Sandra Cisneros

34. This episodic book tells us a great deal about Esperanza's personality. Based on several episodes, summarize what you have learned about the child.

A Separate Peace Test

Name _____

1. Explain whether or not Gene Forrester is a reliable narrator.

2. The events of the novel are largely conveyed via _____.

3. What is Leper's function in this novel?

4. Why is it unimportant to Finny that others know he broke the school's swimming record?

5. Novels often include more than one climax. In your opinion, what is the most climactic moment in the book?

6. Why do you suppose John Knowles set this novel against a background of World War II?

7. Would you rather have Gene or Finny as a close friend? Explain.

8. Explain why Finny opens the Winter Carnival by burning a copy of the *Iliad*.

9. Why is it ironic that the Carnival ends with the news of Leper's telegram telling Gene about his escape from the army?

10. Why is Gene so unfeeling to Leper when he visits Leper at his home?

11. What does Brinker mean when he calls both Leper and Finny casualties?

12. Explain why Gene, not Finny, is unquestionably the novel's protagonist.

13. Why, in your opinion, does Finny fall a second time?

14. Mr. Hadley has a definite opinion about World War II. What do you think of his attitude to the war?

15. Read this thematic statement about the novel from a previous student. Explain why it is an appropriate statement of theme:

> What this novel so wonderfully communicates is
> that envy will destroy even the closest of friendships.

16. Why do you think this novel continues to be universally popular among readers of all ages and in all walks of life?

Poetry Unit Test

Name _____

Some of the poetry you will need to refer to is attached to the back of the test.

1–10: Name the poetic device in the following lines from poetry we have studied.

1. All the world's a stage
    And all the men and women merely players. . ..

2. . . . Whether 'tis nobler in the mind to suffer
    The slings and arrows of outrageous fortune
    Or to take arms against a sea of troubles. . ..

3. A boat with a furled sail at rest in a harbor.

4. Like the leaves of the forest when Summer is green,
    That host with their banners at sunset were seen:
    Like the leaves of the forest when Autumn hath blown,
    That host on the morrow lay withered and strown. . ..

5. . . . . golden daffodils...
    Fluttering and dancing in the breeze.

6. I heard a Fly buzz—when I died. . ..
    With Blue—uncertain stumbling Buzz. . ..

7. I saw a crowd,
    A host of golden daffodils. . ..
    Ten thousand saw I at a glance. . ..

8. I wandered lonely as a cloud. . ..

9. With how sad steps, O Moon, thou climb'st the skies....

10. Life's but a walking shadow, a poor player
    That struts and frets his hour upon the stage. . ..

"Miss Rosie"

11. What does the speaker of this poem imply about Miss Rosie's past and present circumstances?

12. Why is the speaker so impressed by Miss Rosie"?

"The courage that my mother had"

13. What main idea does the poet convey in this poem? Briefly explain how the idea is vividly conveyed.

"Abandoned Farmhouse"

14. The poem does not allow us to definitely decide why the family left the farm in such haste. Some clues within the poem allow us to speculate about this family. What conclusions can we tentatively reach about the husband and wife? How do we know that the family abandoned the farmhouse in some haste?

"Oh, when I was in love with you"

15. Summarize the young man's experience that this poem describes. Identify the poet's tone.

"Sea Fever"

16. Summarize the personality and main desire of the speaker in John Masefield's poem. How does the poet's choice of meter convey this desire?

"The Children and Sir Nameless"

17. What is the main character trait of "Sir Nameless"?

18. Why is the nobleman's name ironic?

19. What is the <u>central</u> irony of Hardy's poem?

20. In your opinion, what is an appropriate way to ensure one is remembered after death?

"Ozymandias"

21. Who was Ozymandias?

22. What does Ozymandias have in common with "Sir Nameless"?

23. Explain how the poetic devices in the last lines of Shelley's poem convey the futility of Ozymandias's intent:

> Round the decay
> Of that colossal wreck, boundless and bare
> The lone and level sands stretch far way.

"The Eagle"

24. How does Tennyson convey the bird's majesty and power in this brief poem?

"A Poison Tree"

25. What important truth is contained in Blake's poem?

"First Fig"

26. Provide a prose summary of Edna St. Vincent Millay's poem "First Fig."

"The Destruction of Sennacherib"

27. Which of God's attributes does this poem convey? Briefly explain how Byron infers this attribute.

Printed in the United States
By Bookmasters